Off *to* Serve

Richard Galentino

Richard Galentino

ILLUSTRATED BY
Paola Bertolini Grudina

HiddenSpring

Jacket, caseside, and book design by Lynn Else

Library of Congress Cataloging-in-Publication Data

Galentino, Richard.
   Off to serve / Richard Galentino ; illustrated by Paola Bertolini Grudina.
     p. cm.
   ISBN 978-1-58768-056-4 (alk. paper)
   1. Voluntarism—Religious aspects—Christianity. I. Title.
   BR115.V64G35 2010
   253´.7—dc22

                                   2009042615

Published in the United States by
HiddenSpring
an imprint of Paulist Press
997 Macarthur Boulevard
Mahwah, New Jersey 07430

www.hiddenspringbooks.com

Printed and bound in Shenzhen, China
by Shenzhen Donnelley Printing Co. Ltd.
March 2010

We are proud of you!

To: _____

From: _____

Congratulations! Act I was a success!

You are now accomplished, celebrated, heralded, and even credentialed.

Now, what will you do?

You could settle down and do more of the same:
clock into a cubicle or go and seek fame,
run to Wall Street for riches,
or decode reality game glitches;
but you're not passionate about that.

WALL STREET

LAW SCHOOL

CALL TO SERVICE

MBA

CUBICLE CENTRAL

And *you*, you're a different kind of cat!

So, be off to serve!

Volunteer, teach, donate, create, care, contribute, build, help,
lift-up, develop, give back, and make a difference in the world.

You'll have to consider the facts,
and form multiple prong attacks.
You might give a person a fish and feed him for a day;
possibly recalculate your length of stay,
begin to teach fishing and put dependency at bay.

Neither charity nor justice alone will suffice,
true service requires sacrifice.

A persistent problem can be a persistent pest.

A simple solution is often the best.

Other problems are greater than the net—
of local people to be met,

and may require you to go upstream,
and join a global team.

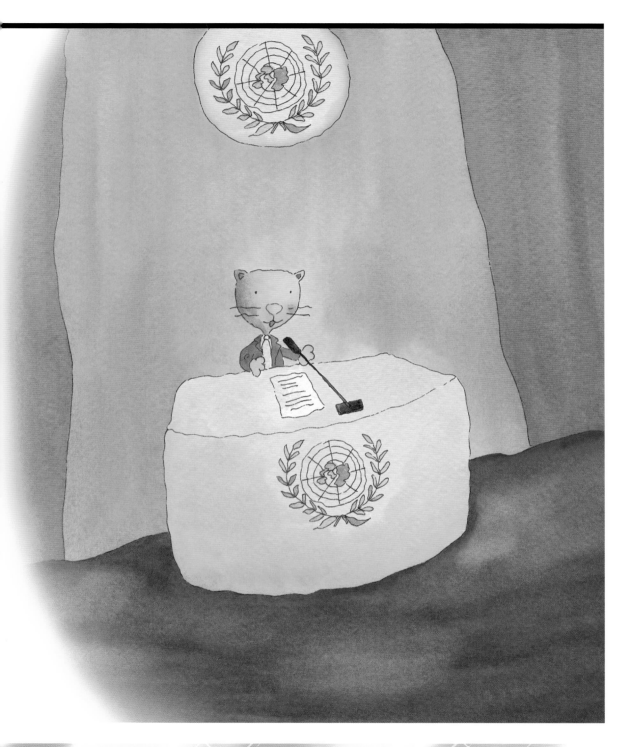

And if problems persist—and they will—
look for a win-win,
rather than a spin-spin.

You may have to listen at the grass roots,
or go to the top of the chutes;
collaborate with CEOs and *campesinos*,
middle class masses and students taking classes,
presidents and residents,
policy makers and movers and shakers.

Wear the appropriate clothes for each group.
Be truthful, fair, and keep everybody in the loop.

While the path is dusty and less
traveled on the journey of service,
be assured and not nervous;
many mentors, saints, and sages are in
the distance,
and await you at this very instance.

Other experiments with truth can be found
in books;
it may require more than a few looks.

At times you may grow weary and leery,
  misused and confused,
  tired and depressed,
  burned-out and without clout.

You'll have to meditate and contemplate,
reorganize and prioritize,
rest and relax,
play and pray.

If you're empty, you'll have nothing to give.
It won't be easy.

Before helping others, you'll have to help yourself—
something not selfish at all,
and necessary when answering your inner call.

By following your call
you'll receive more than you give.
Be thankful; immerse yourself in the
community,
and fully live.

Forgetting who is serving who,
you'll be accompanying each other
in lieu of lining up in the great social
status queue.

You'll learn the language, dialect, slang, and twang.
Eat the same food, celebrate the same triumphs, and mourn
the same losses.
You may have to battle apathy, stubbornness, malaria,
or resistance to change beyond measure—
far from the safety of software-simulated adventure.

Whether embarking for a day, week, year, or lifetime,
take time to discover and discern your vocation—
where your talents and deepest desire trump today's crushing
needs and envision tomorrow's collaborative world.

And what you give up—
whether a big boat or fancy coat,
wall plaques or fat stacks,
golf game at par or fast car—
won't really be a sacrifice at all
because you'll be following your call.

Your skills can augment local wisdom in distant lands and serve peoples of various clans...

...or *solve* challenges in your own backyard
easy to ignore—
like the poor.

Don't let your hopes and dreams swerve.
Be off to serve!

Change yourself and the world for the better,
just don't forget to send home a letter.

In the world of making a difference
you are among the brightest few.

Be assured, we are proud of you.

Find volunteer opportunities, post your reflections on service, share this book with a friend, read stories from the field, link to other service organizations, and participate in the growing global volunteer service movement at:

offtoserve.org

The best way to find yourself is to lose yourself in the service of others.
—Mohandas K. Gandhi